AFTERHIPHOP.COM PRESENTS

JAILHOUSE TALK

NAVIGATING THE SYSTEM FROM LOCKUP TO E.O.S.

RAUL MEDINA

CONTENTS

ACKNOWLEDGEMENT & THANKS

Many humble thanks and much gratitude to all who have stood beside me, who have continued to lift me up, and who had my back at my lowest time in life. All of you are truly the champions. You are the superstars. To my counselors, spiritual healers, holistic doctors, physical therapists, historians and all my love ones I call my psychiatrists. (lol) But, no joke. For real for real for putting up with my crazy ass for so many years and never giving up on me.

Omar Islam, Florida Chapter: My brother you have left an impression on my soul and life. When I was a free man, you were there for me helping guide me in all the preparation and development of Hoodstock Music Fest. The event that forever changed the music scene in Miami-Wynwood. You continually to pointed me in the right direction. I salute you Bro. You visited me in 3 different institutions in the state of Florida. You bought my son Raoulito shoes when I was locked up. You sat on the corner of my Mother's bed and listened to her pain. You even went as far as sneaking a pair of sneakers into the Department of Corrections on a visit once. High-risk entertainment!! You were there when I got off the Greyhound bus and put a few dollars in my pocket. You even organized for me and Pitbull to have a chess tournament. I deeply regret missing that chess game, but I am still very grateful. In this space and time, I send good vibrations your way. Salute!

El Moab, AKA Smooth Sinista Class: Straight up King, I take my hat off to you. Your name proceeds your reputation, taking us all to school. Schooling humanity and schooling ME into becoming the best human being I can be. You are an awesome business partner. Your wisdom is greatly appreciated.

Wheels, my brother from another mother: When I came home almost 14 years ago, I was able to earn funds to pay my bills because of you. It was a rough time for me. You didn't know who I was, yet you opened doors for me. A lot of car doors, that is. (lol) I could never let another man cry in my ear about how hard it is. No one went through the belly of the beast and knows pain like me and you. So, when someone starts to cry over some bullshit, I show them the real struggle. I tell them they really don't know what pain is. I say, "Let me tell you story about Wheels and *his* pain so you can learn how to get motivated."

Raoul M. Medina, my youngest son: I give thanks to The Most High for you. When I was assed out in the mix, with nowhere to go, you lifted me up. You even came down to my level and helped me run www.TheBestAutoDetailer.com!! It was tough work, and all I can say is thanks for sharing the struggle with me.

Raoul A. R. Medina, my oldest son: Thank you for Noah Medina, my first grandson. You are always finding a way to keep us connected with the cosmos. As we grow as a family, we find out that we as a people are all victims. Again, thanks for being more than a son. Your knowledge goes beyond this world. The family guru!! The very best thing is knowing we are like-minded.

Anna Medina, my sister: Thanks for never turning your back on me. You have always kept shit real. Respect to you and all your children: Natasha, DJ, and Mel Perez.

To the Whyte Family: Mr. Whyte, I can say you are the best thing our family has with your patience, smooth talk, and awesome jokes. You keep our family smiling, loaded with lots of wisdom, and continue to carry our family to levels unheard. I thank you for always encouraging us to continue chasing our dreams and aspirations and you are always supporting our businesses. You are amazing! All I can say is, when I grow up, I want to be just like you. Ms. Betty, the healer of the family: Anytime (or anywhere), if we get sick physically, mentally, or spiritually, you are a warrior ready for the battle. Thank you. Brother Yusef Whyte: mad love brother! Thanks for always having my back. Shellene Whyte: Shelly, thanks for all your encouraging words. You are an awesome sister, wife and mother. Haneefah Whyte: never stop chasing your dreams.

Najeebah A. Medina: you are truly the blessing to this family and to me. I've always had willpower, but because of you, I know how to channel it. You keep me healthy. You are always telling me how great I am when I'm feeling down or feeling sorry for myself. You always come with the words that uplifts me. Bless up, The Hemp Goddess. I am in love with you. Zakiyah E. N. Medina and Salah N. Medina: You are my world, my life. You give me reason to rise every day to do my very best to design a better world for you to live in.

A good vibration to all the holistic doctors in my life: Dr. BaBa Pearsun, thank you so much for healing me when I thought I wasn't going to make it. Dr. Love, thank you for showing us how to keep our organs healthy. CHI GONG MASTER Dr. Galloway of Herbal Gardens, we give thanks for your contribution to the holistic community. Dr. Colon, our pediatric physician. Rest in Power to Dr. Sebi, and big ups to all your family continuing to heal humanity; along with Mrs. Dr. Sebi (Mrs. Patsy B. Bowman), who critiqued my edibles. Providing me with healthier ideas by adding sea moss to **RAW HEMP EDIBLES**. Rest in Power to our midwife, Becky, for allowing me to deliver my last seed and giving me the skills to bring life in. We honor you and raise up the heavens for you. Dr. Anita Jones, from Each One Teach One. We love you.

And let me give a shout out to the artists I've been working with: Mr. Grim 2Da Reapa, King Yudah, Moonshyne Brown, Infinite Mind, DJ Heron, Serum 305 and The Hemp Goddess. You all keep me creating; the key to staying young and alive. Rhonda Fleming, thanks for helping me find my words.

INTRODUCTION

Greetings! Before jumping into this manual, I would like to introduce myself. I am Raúl Medina, AKA Legendary DJ Raw Miami. I have a well-known reputation throughout Florida, but I am most significantly known for spearheading and establishing the culture of Hip-Hop in South Florida. I am the originator of the Hip-Hop Jam *Hoodstock Music Festival*. Established in 1994, it was a massive, one-of-a-kind event.

Early life for me began in NYC, the Bronx. Back in the 70's, it was common for young men to be a part of a gang to rep his hood. As the nephew of a high-ranking Ching-Ga-Ling in a well-known motorcycle biker gang, I had no choice. I was grandfathered in. I can remember selling dope as early as the age of 7 or 8. At that age, did I know what I was doing? No, but watching skulls being cracked to white meat taught me quickly to pay attention and not mess up. That's exactly what I did and became a natural in the game. Around this time, the Bronx was also giving birth to "The Jam". There were 4 Elements: the DJ, the B-Boy, the Graffiti Artist, and the MC. There is no denying The Jam helped shape the entire landscape of Hip-Hop. Some gangs actually became dance crews battling instead of gang-banging. As an adolescent, I was dead center in the middle of the action watching Hip-Hop begin to grow and evolve.

Always a loyal fan of Hip-Hop from the beginning, I saw there was a void for the culture when we moved down to Miami. In the 70's as well as very early 80's, disco ruled the airwaves. Hip-Hop was the new kid on the block and was changing music as we knew it, right in front of our eyes. By the time *Hoodstock Music Festival* was coming to fruition, I was the next "Big Boy" (slang for a successful drug dealer) in Wynwood. Of course, I loved everything about having endless funds. But with no goals, no dreams or real aspirations, I was just hood rich. As a member of a family in the life, I was conditioned to believe going to prison was a part of life. We all could expect to go at least once. When things got hot, we were programmed to protect our upline. Oh, the promises of perks while you do your time! Soon after sentencing, however, you learn everyone has turned their backs on you. I'm breaking bread with you right now because I want you to feel me. I want you to know I am just like you. I've been through some shit in my life. My fate was that of many successful drug dealers. First is the flight, then there's the fall. Prison.

My primary goal with this handbook is to share some knowledge I gained over the course of my two sentences. Knowledge I wished I had prior to being introduced to "the system". There really is only one way to do a "successful" prison term. From the very start, you must begin to change your attitude. Plain and simple. I probably would've had far better results had I been better equipped. Of course, there is some type of rehabilitation program available in all correctional facilities. However, what I found missing from these programs was a lack of promoting personal development that could empower the convict. Giving or returning power to the convict is uplifting. This could help arm them with tools so they can stay home, stay free, and never go back.

My first prison term was in the early 1980's. One of the toughest to do time as it was still a part of the chain gang era. It was hard work but during the 80's, the State of Florida still paid convicts for labor. Inmates were still fed quite well (we were eating T-bones with broccoli and corn on the cob), plus we got $10 per week!! I had been sentenced to one year and a day. Almost sounds cute, doesn't it? Nothing could be further from that. "One year and a day" meant NO probation. The months went by, I served my time and then rounded out the decade by keeping my nose clean. And then came the 90's.

Never will I say I was completely innocent. God knows I did my dirt. As a matter of fact, I had done enough dirt to catch the eye of an aspiring politician. Running for mayor at the time, he would attempt to use me and my case as a springboard to spur his career forward. The events of my case caused a stir in the media, thus making it a high-profile case. When I began to see how much attention the media gave my case, I found that to be a huge head-scratch. High-profile? My case? I guess with the reputation DJ Raw & the K.O.P. (Knock Out Posse) had as a well-known criminal organization based out of the Miami Wynwood area, I could easily be used for political theatre. The media did such a great job, I began to believe the persona they assigned me. I was donned the "Godfather of Miami's Hip-Hop Culture". Of course, I'm not trying to grandstand. I merely want to set the tone for the climate surrounding my court case.

As aforementioned, my sentence in the 80's was different from my sentence in the 90's. Long gone were the days inmates were paid for their labor. The 1990's brought a burgeoning of privatized prisons and hefty limitations to state and federal budgets for detention centers. Upon arrival at a detention facility, an inmate now received 3 uniforms, 3 pairs of socks, a bath towel, a wash towel, and a pair of shower slides. Oh, and yes, mandatory labor with no monetary benefit. The only thing that got paid was the inmate's debt to society.

Although my case had been labeled high-profile, the case was still considered non-violent. Frequently, inmates are separated by their criminal offenses. There are no absolutes concerning this practice, but oddly enough, I had been assigned to one of the 8 cells on the 6th floor of the "House of Pain" Dade County Jail. The reason this was significant is because this location was typically assigned to murderers and killers. Prosecutors were really trying to make an example of me. To give some context, I shared the floor with the likes of Juan Carlos Chavez. The Jimmy Ryce case garnered national media attention due to the gruesome nature of Chavez's heinous crimes. When I first became acquainted with him, I had no clue about the details of his crime. What I did know was he had no help from the outside. Thankfully, I was fortunate enough to have a saint of a mother, Maria Sepulveda, who was able to shoot me $20 every now and then. I can remember the time some inmates were able to get into Chavez's cell and beat him mercilessly. They pummeled him so badly he had to be transferred to an outside hospital for care. It's been 20 years and I sometimes can still hear his haunting screams from that beating. It left such an imprint on me that when my mother visited me following the incident, I asked if she could send him a little help. Bless up to the heavens for my mother. She looked out for him by sending him some funds and even purchasing him clothes for his court appearance. The trial is how we found out what he had done. My mother and I were horrified. Then I was angry. My anger prompted me to demand a reason for why he did it. I pointedly asked him, "What made you do it?!" His only answer was the evil one had overtaken him and he blanked out. He said he couldn't remember doing anything so horrible.

Telling you about this macabre memory has a purpose. I told you earlier this handbook's purpose is to give some survival tips and assist in navigating some common struggles and pitfalls when you are placed in the system. That story I recanted told of an inmate who didn't have a support system on the outside. By the contrast, I *did* have help. But even with help, it can be a tough road ahead. I was sentenced and next thing I knew, I was on a bus wondering just how my 5'5"-119-pound-self got there. So many things were running through my mind. Being sentenced to 10 years, I knew there was no way I could get back in the game once I got out. The underground couldn't take a chance on me again; I had been "compromised". I had to get my shit together and have a plan. Like myself, I realized there are thousands of brothers and sisters in desperate need of guidance before they are released.

After hearing numerous discouraging remarks about their plight, such as "No one will hire you, you're an ex-con", some positivity and encouragement is a necessary boost to the psyche.

Assistance after lockup can be found, but what about the start of your sentence? How can you prepare? For example, you've been charged, and granted bail... can you make bail? And out on bail, do you know how best to spend time while waiting for trial? Is there anyway to be productive and proactive if you are unable to make bail?

Securing your support system on the outside is extremely helpful while inside. When you are facing a prison term, it can be a daunting and scary time. But it's time to turn that fear into courage. Take your opportunity to turn the negative energy into positive.

CHAPTER I

Changing one's mindset is paramount to attaining success. While I was afraid of what lay ahead of me, I somehow knew I had to connect to The Source, my Higher Power. I knew finding my higher self would change my journey. Because I did have help from my mother, I had the chance to further my education during my sentence. I was 33 years old and was determined to receive my G.E.D. along with any and all certificates and licenses I could acquire. When they say, you can't teach an old dog new tricks, that is a lie. Work hard. Work harder. Work like your life depends on it, because it does.

While you may gain some valid connections on the inside, this is not the time for making friends. Sharing your innermost thoughts with others can be detrimental, so channeling your energy inward is best anyway. Staying closed off socially can be a challenge. Many times, it results in compartmentalizing, and faking it till you make it. It would be nice to have an outlet for all the anxiety bottled up. Unfortunately, because resources are limited, only inmates with specific criminal charges are assigned mental health programs.

If you have been charged with a drug crime, many times the judge will include participation in a drug rehabilitation program as a part of the sentencing. The state bases eligibility on the type of offender. Those who fit the criteria for the program get evaluated for admission by assessment questions. If all hours allocated for the drug rehab program have been used, usually an inmate cannot participate in this program again. (These inmates have previously served time and have exhausted the hours available for this program.) For those charged with crimes involving mental defect, psychological and psychiatric therapy is included as a part of their sentence. If you are able to get assistance through any of these programs, take advantage of all resources available.

Maintaining a low profile is a plus for many inmates. It is always most beneficial to listen more than you speak. Being self-confident but respectful to others is important. If you project you are pre-occupied with personal goals and focused on self-improvement, it is rare you will be disturbed. There is a tacit, unspoken sort of respect among inmates for a brother or a sister who is disciplined and bettering themselves.

Figuring out your interests can help you with the direction you should take when choosing your work assignments. Again, on the state level, there is mandatory labor with no pay, but there are ways to gain some small benefits. From the very start, navigating the legal system can be treacherous. If you are arrested and charged, you will wait in jail until you are able to go before a judge for arraignment. An arraignment is a summons to court to answer for a criminal charge. Unless it is a weekend, and if you are eligible, bail is usually offered about 24 hours after you have been booked and processed. The decision as to whether you are granted or denied bail can be influenced by the arresting officer, or decided solely by the judge presiding over your case.

At my first arraignment, I was denied bail. It took several court appearances with a judge (including a month in solitary confinement) before I was granted bail. Several of my co-defendants had been granted bail. Ironically, when I was finally granted the opportunity to make bail, I couldn't pay it. I could not afford cover the bail amount.

The bail process can be handled in two ways: self-pay, or through a bail bondsman. Now, if you got it like that, go ahead and bond out. Pay the full amount in its entirety and not be on the hook for anyone. However, if using a bail bondsman, know that you must pay 10% of the bail amount given in the court ruling. For example, if it is $10K and under, 10% is all that is required. If the bond amount is more than $10K, the bail bondsman will ask for collateral to secure your loan amount. (In most cases, persons put their homes up or other assets as the collateral). As an example, my bond was $500K. 10% of $500K would be $50K. I couldn't afford to post that amount so I had no choice but to stay in. If you are unable to make bail, don't worry. This isn't the end of the road for you.

When you can't afford bail, they will set a follow-up trial arraignment date to see if you then are able to bond out. It behooves the state to continue to set a number of trial arraignments to coax an inmate to take a plea deal. The simple reason is cost. Trials are expensive. The amount taxpayers are saddled with in criminal trials can be offset if an inmate takes a plea. If no plea is accepted, you will be transferred to a holding facility until you take a plea deal, or until a trial date has been set. In a worst-case scenario, I've seen an inmate with a murder charge kept in county lock-up for 5 years. That is extreme but entirely possible. I do want you to keep in mind, if you take a plea deal, you won't be able to revise or amend any details and/or evidence in your case. Don't box yourself into a situation you can't fix. Each case is different, just try to navigate the system equipped with knowledge. This is why, in many cases, going to trial may be the best-case scenario.

Regardless of your financial situation, what funds you do have, you should be smart and use them wisely. One of my co-defendants made bail with the last funds he had, only to return and endure the nightmare of processing all over again 90 days later. I will be honest with you, most heads who fall are already on probation or already out on bond. These cats probably already know the jailhouse rules: jump out before you go in front of a judge. You don't want to find yourself in front of a judge, already in jail, being arraigned on another charge. You'll only be making things harder for yourself.

If you know you have to ride, make sure you put your funds to work FOR you. In the case of my co-defendant, he had to come up with $7K to bond out. As a home owner, he was able to use his house as collateral. Since it was the 90's, mortgage rates were excellent. His payments were only $700/month. If he could have thought long term, he would've seen his house could provide income, as opposed to becoming an additional bill (bail). He could have opted to collect rent using a trusted family member, or maybe hiring a property manager. The rent could be an amount that would cover the mortgage as well as maintenance of the home. He could be financially secure and have somewhere to live upon release. Not to oversimplify the entire process, but he really could have been set. He bonded out and placed himself in a financial hole. After he couldn't maintain his mortgage payments, his home went into foreclosure and his credit rating went down the drain. All I'm saying is be wise about the use of your money. Make it make sense.

A hustler already has a go-getter mentality. For all purposes intended, a hustler is an entrepreneur. Why not make the hustle legal? You can do this by starting an LLC or an S-Corporation to legitimize your enterprise. But *why* do you need a business? When you jump, finding a job after doing time can be a huge challenge. Of course, anything is possible. However, the odds are assuredly more in your favor if you work for yourself. I was blessed to already have an LLC before I went inside. To this day, I can proudly say I still have the same Limited Liability Corporation I established in 1994: Hoodstock, LLC. It was definitely a life saver when I got out.

While out on bail, you can try to set up your LLC or S-Corp (this is what the IRS calls a small business corporation. You may need help deciding which of these is right for you). If you are already doing time, you will need a trusted partner to assist you in setting one of these up. A professional would be best, but that has a fee associated with it. It could be a family member or a close friend but they must be TRUSTED. This trust can be scarce and hard to find. At the toughest time, when you need to call on people, no one is around. It will appear you have zero friends, and unfortunately, many times family isn't much better. My ex-wife showed me just how selfish family can get. How swiftly heads can turn green on you. She forged my name on documents and proceeded to take all the insurance money on MY home and party it all away. She even moved some cat into the very same home she and I shared when SWAT came and knocked down doors and dragged me out. We had been married for 10 years, yet I was betrayed so easily. This sounds pretty major, but hey, even getting family just to write you a letter while you are serving a sentence is like pulling teeth. But that is a subject for a different time.

If you are not granted bail or cannot afford to post bail, you can still set yourself up to be in a good position upon release. Setting up an LLC with your state is usually no more than $100-$150 to start. You should begin this process as soon as possible. The Articles of Organization, laws and rules can vary from state to state. Certain funding can be available to help your fledgling business if you meet lending institutions' requirements. For example, in the state of Florida, small business loans can be given to corporations established at least 3 months. If you're already serving your sentence, it may be best to begin organizing this at least 6 months before you jump. Having a loyal partner to help you begin this is priceless. It can make the difference for you in the game of life. You may have to contend with a few maintenance fees, but no trouble with Uncle Sam. Businesses that are dormant, with no activity and not making any money don't accrue taxes.

These aren't hard and fast rules to follow, I'm just trying to put you onto a little game that helped me get free and be self-sufficient. Everyone will have their own personal journey to travel. Let's just get you some tools to make it a little bit easier.

CHAPTER II

A little earlier in this handbook, I made mention of my stature. I'm not physically imposing, so of course, I was a little nervous about going inside. No matter what, I knew had to be focused. No distractions, including attracting bad energies and bad actors. Even if it is your first time doing a bid, you must keep it together. Mental fortitude helps you keep your wits about you at all times. It's easier said than done, but don't be afraid. I always say fear stands for False Evidence Appearing Real. Don't get me wrong, the danger is real. I'm saying don't *create* more danger in your head. When you feel yourself creating scenarios, STOP! The mind is a powerful asset if used correctly. It's only natural to have some anxiety about the situation. But I'm going to tell you what worked for me.

By nature, being imprisoned with others can be a hostile environment; yet, keeping your composure and asserting yourself (while NOT being an asshole) is possible. I actually spent the first 3 years of my sentence in solitary confinement. 36 months in the hole. 4,380 days. That can take a toll on the mental. I cried. I broke down and cried profusely. And while I cried, I didn't know who I was praying to but I knew there was a Source, a Power higher than me. I prayed to The Most High to protect and guide me on this journey as I walked directly into the belly of the beast. I pleaded with The Most High to guide me and to show me the path I needed to take. Spiritual affirmations give you the confidence that things will be fine. Some words from The Good Book I kept at the front of my mind are found at Matthew 7:7-8: "*Ask, and it shall be given to you; seek, and you shall find; knock, and it shall be opened unto you: For every one that asks, receives; and he/she that seeks, finds. And to him/her that knocks, it shall be opened.*" I won't go into detail, but shortly after I learned and continued to recite this prayer, I got real reassurance that everything was going to be alright. EVERYONE who asks shall receive. No exceptions. In my years of searching and discovery, I found what is referred to as Universal Law. Whether you define it by that term or another, Universal Law is for everyone. We all benefit from the use of this power gifted to humanity by The Most High. Of course, I continued sharpening my relationship with The Most High even after my sentence ended. It has evolved and deepened. My spiritual support system came through the assistance of a few profound motivating speakers such as Les Brown, Jim Rohn, Jerry Clark, Danny Johnson, Tony Robbins, Louise Hayes, and so many more who brought me to this truth. And there is no way I could ever forget to mention my wife and partner, Najeebah, of 14 years who was also instrumental in helping me develop in a spiritual way. Planted seeds of spirituality must be watered and cultivated. It is a never-ending practice to remain sharp. In reading Claude Bristol's book, **The Magic of Believing**, I was further educated about the power of good and evil and how we can use Universal Law in this way. But know this, if you use this power for evil, it is sure to come back the same way. That's what has been defined by Hindus and Buddhists as karma. What you do comes back to you.

You will notice changes within yourself as you grow spiritually. The longer you implement the practice of being spiritually centered, it becomes evident to others on the outside. Being diligent and dutifully distracted keeps you out of trouble and off the radar of troublemakers. You won't even see trouble because it won't be near you. This happened in my case. Once I decided to stay focused, I never really saw fights anymore. I didn't even really get bad vibes, or even a nasty look. I was virtually invisible. I was physically present, but I had spiritually and mentally elevated out of that place. I was often invited to play sports, play cards, even gamble, but I would gracefully decline and bow out. I always had an excuse, a little white lie, to get out of the request. "Wow, thanks but I'm writing home." "I'd love to but I'm working on my case in the law library." "Wish I could, but I've got to study for a test." Soon it was clear I had a different agenda while serving my time. This technique worked for me and I remained unbothered.

So, in short order, I am not giving you a sales pitch on church or religion. I am stating a lot can be gained from knowing one's self. When you feel the positivity within, it can't help but spill over into other aspects of your life. Feeding your spirituality is where you will find the power to keep living, the power to move forward, and the power to forgive yourself. Feeling good about one's self even helps your work ethic. This in turn builds responsibility and an increase in pride in yourself. After a while, it will become noticeable to all.

CHAPTER III

Your road to achieving success has got to be two-fold. You've got to avoid the pitfalls of trouble, of course. Keeping your mind occupied is just as important as staying physically active, too. I previously spoke on the availability of enrichment and certificate programs. I advise taking advantage of anything and everything that interests you. This is prime opportunity to look at this situation as a way to center your attention solely on self. While serving my second sentence (10 years), I received well over 50 certifications for completing various courses of study. Prior to enrolling in these programs, the furthest I had completed in school was an 8th grade education in Bridgeport, CT. Once my family and I returned to NYC, OGs and the streets became my teachers. Going inside was finally my chance to develop some self-discipline.

If you don't pay attention to anything else I say, I simply suggest to make the best use of your time. Time itself is the most valuable thing you will ever have. Once it is lost, it is never recovered. The old saying "An idle mind is the Devil's Workshop" is true. If you find you have idle time, try to fill it with being more productive.

When you first arrive, most institutions will give you a questionnaire to get a better assessment of the level of your education. Usually they'll want to know if you completed high school and graduated with a diploma, or if you already have a trade. Even if you didn't graduate, they may want to know how what level you completed. Based on your history and resume, they are already planning a course of action for your work detail. If it has not already been achieved, some prisons make it mandatory to receive a G.E.D. (For those who do not wish to enroll, usually their work assignments are the most undesirable.) Enrollment in various programs can occur almost immediately after arrival. Trustees are the liaison used to interview and question new inmates seeking to sign up for different programs. There are no restrictions for enrollment. The only challenge is when programs are full and no available slots. There are also no restrictions when it comes to taking programs concurrently. If you can handle the workload, you can sign up.

Sometimes your educational programs can give you a little respite in the summer time! A huge percentage of detention centers have NO air conditioning. Finding yourself in a cool learning environment versus being in a sweatbox sounds like winning to me. Perhaps you would be interested in signing up for access to the law library. It's open to everyone. You can take some time to review your own case and those similar to yours. Who knows? You may find some clerical errors that could make a big difference in your case's evidence.

In addition to keeping busy, finding like-minded individuals to associate with is another aid in staying on track and maintaining accountability. Having someone who asks what you are working on or how your last test went can be encouraging. Iron sharpens iron. Everything you do should be with the mindset to help you get further along with your goals.

CHAPTER IV

When an inmate arrives at a detention center, the State provides each inmate with basic necessities: 3 meals a day, soap, shampoo, toothpaste, and 2 towels. Any extras outside of this will be the inmate's expense.

There are many inmates without outside help. It could be due to a number of reasons. Maybe they've burned bridges with family and exhausted their credibility with them. Or maybe they just don't want to burden them with their expenses. Whatever the case, if you can't get what you want and need from the outside, practice self-discipline and go without. Those without self-control find themselves in the kind of trouble you don't want.

There is always someone hustling in the dorm by running a canteen or a mini-commissary. Getting a loaner with these guys is usually 1 for 2. Meaning, if you get a pack of cigarettes, you'll have to pay back TWO packs. This can bring a world of trouble for you. If you do have outside help, my recommendation is to simply wait until your funds land. Virtual accounts can be set up for the inmate to access monies given to them from the outside. The money is accessed with a code assigned to the inmate. There is also a similar account set up for inmates for phone calls. This can vary based on facility. County jail and state or federal prisons have different systems for these resources. I just want to say the guy running the canteen is an opportunist, like a loan shark. Loans inside are always a set-up. Bet on it.

That phrase brings me to another rule: **No Gambling!!** The sports change with the seasons, from professional football to college March Madness to NBA Finals to boxing/MMA matches. All these can be quite entertaining but just as dangerous for you. Simple card games among friend-lies have resulted in brawls over the dumbest shit I've ever seen. I can promise you this, if a pack of cigarettes or coffee is involved, the head cracking will commence when payment is not received for your debts. Stay away from gambling. It doesn't end happily.

I've talked a little bit about my past and my family affiliation. I came from a long line of gang bangers, some of who did some real time. I was also comfortably acquainted with quite a few of the officers at DFC (Florida Department of Corrections in Florida City). When it came to getting anything from the outside brought in, I could've been the MAN. I made some guys pretty upset because I refused to bring drugs or contraband inside. I chose instead to bring in sneakers around the holidays. Or I would sell my "happy meals", yellow rice $5 a plate. Whatever I would choose to do, I kept it clean.

To help you gain some small personal benefits, choose your work assignments wisely. It can be the channel for your "clean hustle", an equal bartering and trading with other inmates to get what you need. For example, getting a job in the chow hall can bring a quick little benefit. Having extra food can work to your advantage in a trade with other inmates. If you are unable to land a job in the chow hall, another suggestion would be the laun-dry room. The majority of inmates that have outside help typically have visi-tors. When it's time for visitation, they'll want their uniforms cleaned & pressed for the visitor's park. You could barter something for your laundry services. If by chance you have visitors, there are definite ways to move your funds. Many times, the ladies can pay off/trade on your behalf at the visiting park. This isn't me condoning rule-breaking, this is me telling you how it goes down in the dorm. The guards know bartering/trading is common practice among inmates, they just look the other way. It's all up to how you choose to stay afloat. Being able to have a clean hustle by way of your work assignment can give you a little more breathing room and time for enrichment programs.

CHAPTER V

I have stressed how important it is for you to keep your wits about you and stay mentally healthy. When you are taking care of your mind, you should figure out how to take care of your physical body as well. You already know your resources are limited and access to a full variety of foods and nutrition is pretty much non-existent. But you don't have to succumb to poor habits just because you are inside.

When I first arrived, my diet was shit. I basically ate a honey bun and drank a coke every single day for about 3 years. I went from weighing about 119-122 lbs all the way up to 210. Nothing but butt and gut. I had fallen into an extremely unhealthy lifestyle and it affected me by causing high blood pressure and the dreadful chronic disease diabetes. I eventually had to take a trip to the infirmary and the nurse formally gave me the diagnosis. She asked me how long my sentence was and when I told her, she replied, "If you don't lose 50 pounds, you won't make it." I really felt sorry for myself. But I learned the condition could be controlled by managing my diet. I got busy pretty quickly. I eliminated almost all sugar right away. I began drinking a diet coke instead of a regular coke to manage some of my sugar intake. I didn't add sugar to my coffee. Another sacrifice that really hurt was giving up my Snickers and Three Musketeers candy bars. But this was a small price to pay for my wealth. Health IS wealth. My right-hand man had the same shitty diet as I did but he ignored the advice of the medical professionals. He didn't change anything and eventually lost BOTH his kidneys, prompting the need for a transplant. Changing your diet is a small price to pay on the grand scale of health matters.

I was dutiful in changing my diet and that brought some weight loss, but I knew I needed to shed some more. During my sentence, I ran across an old friend of mine, Tony Diaz. He was my ex-brother-in-law and always very fit. I thought I'd ask him for some fitness tips. At the top of his list: cardio. He told me I needed to walk at least an hour and a half to begin burning fat. This wasn't a hard practice to start. It was just walking. After a while, I thought it could be fun to run. My first run was NOT fun. I wasn't paying attention to my path and I twisted my ankle badly. I was bummed out because for weeks, I had been committed to my new lifestyle changes and lost a little weight. It all came back when I was down with the injury. But each day, I gave myself a pep talk. I laid on my back in my bunk and told myself, over and over, "You are going to be fine. You are going to win. You are healthy." Whoever chants the most, manifests the most. You can talk yourself into health, freedom, and success. I would even envision myself running.

The moment I was able, I was back at it. I took 30 days to rehab myself to a point I felt my ankle was strong enough for a jog and then a run. I was very proud of myself because I didn't give up on me. Increasing your physical activity will certainly help you trim down. The combination of stepping up my light workout and cutting out sugar was the beginning of my complete lifestyle change.

The meals provided by the state are purported to be nutritious, but usually, they are seriously lacking in that area. Not to mention they lack the appetizing factor. These meals can be high in sodium and sugar, as well as being made with many animal fats and other bi-products. One of the health and lifestyle "hacks" many inmates perform is learning about different faiths and religions. Namely, Judaism and Islam. These two religions have protected rights concerning very specific dietary restrictions. These CANNOT be ignored by the state. Kosher and halal meals must be provided to those who are members of these religions. Unless you have been given a formal diagnosis from the doctor for a particular diet, religious groups are the only inmates allowed special diets. During my quest to enrich my spiritual self, I aligned myself with the teachings of Islam. Transforming my mind, followed by adhering to a beneficial diet to keep my fleshly vessel clean, helped bring a change to my life I would never forget. I adopted the vegan lifestyle and have maintained it for 2 decades. If you are just as selective about what you choose to feed your body as you do your mind, you can be your healthiest self.

CHAPTER VI

Overall, the most significant thing I would like my readers to get from this handbook is acknowledging the value of time. It costs more than anything you'll ever possess. It's why it is taken from those of us who have broken the law. Whether you are doing time or a free person, take care not to ever waste time. Even when I was on the inside, I saw it over and over again. Brothers with no direction falling prey to mindless entertainment and mindless conversation leading to nothing and nowhere fast. But you don't have to succumb to poor habits. Know your worth. Understanding the value of your self-worth can be life-changing. If you are looking to change your life, empower yourself! Equip yourself! Always know the Universe will respond to your thoughts. Thoughts turn into things. Adopting small practices like journaling or creating a vision board can help you with seeing your goals. You visualize so things can materialize in your everyday life.

When you have a plan of action, it is easier to stay on the road to success. Focus has come up many times in this handbook. If you find your focus is fleeting or faltering, finding ways to keep yourself from being sidetracked can come in many forms. I would frequently reference my journal or a quick note jotted down in the margin of my reading material for a simple reset. My quick list of encouraging words can be in found three of my favorite personal empowerment books:

Allen, James. **As a Man Thinketh**. 1903.

Hill, Napoleon. **Think and Grow Rich**. 1937.

Bristol, Claude. **The Magic of Believing**. 1948.

This handbook isn't a complete and exhaustive checklist but hopefully I touched on some things that could ease some anxiety for first-timers, and even recidivists who want to finally get it together. Set yourself up for success. You have a chance to right your wrongs in the eyes of the law, but you also deserve to get yourself right for you and your family. Breaking bad cycles isn't easy, but determination and self-discipline can will you through the storm that lies ahead.

Stay well, stay mindful and stay free.

AUTHOR'S NOTE:

My purpose for putting out this information is to help and give hope to my brothers and sisters. Hope is one of the most powerful desires mankind possesses. Success is another fervent desire of many and I want my brothers and sisters to understand there are many roads to success. Definitely more than one way to skin a cat. We are all on our own journey. For those on a specific mission, one needs to be equipped with the right ammo. Initially, I was on a come-up mission. I was my own worst enemy. I was living for the moment with nothing planned for tomorrow. My big shift came when I learned that everything has a vibration and is energy, negative or positive. Once I accepted that truth, I understood whatever I put out has a return. I became well acquainted with The Law of Attraction. It works. You must "visualize to materialize". Because we are all different, it works differently for each of us. Manifestation has no scheduled time of arrival. It took me 10 years inside and then another 10 years in the free world for the beginnings of my manifestations to arrive. The biggest changes occurred when I began the practice of chanting my desires. I believe he who chants the most will receive the most. I went from barely being able to read when I first went inside, to achieving a number of educational accomplishments. I went from poor personal health habits to being physically fit and a vegan for the past 13 years. I went from unreliable housing to a beautiful home built from the ground up, with whom I share with my beautiful, loving wife and my beautiful children. I went from illegal enterprise to being a legitimately established businessman; owning RAW HEMP EDIBLES, LLC ™©®, 420 BROWARD LLC, & HOODSTOCK LLC (the very same business established c. 1994) This isn't meant to impress you with my accomplishments. I just want to impress upon you that you can do it, too. It can be done in all aspects of life, even down to designing the sort of relationship you desire. I'm not selling dreams. I am saying that if you do the work, you may surprise yourself with what you design. Everyone has their version of success. My idea of success may not be yours, and vice versa. I have made it a point to be a servant of the community in various ways. In the past, I know I put my fair share of madness into the world. Now, I want to be a beacon of light in the darkness for those hopeful of a better life with better days ahead.